I H[...]
QUE[...]
GRANDMA

"Grandma, why do we call the earth our mother?"

"Does your mama feed you, little one?"

2

"So does Mother Earth."

3

"Does your mother give you water, little one?"

4

"So does Mother Earth."

"Does your mother play games with you when the sun warms your back, little one?"

"So does Mother Earth."

"Does your mother sing you
soft songs when the sun sinks low,
little one?"

8

"So does Mother Earth."

9

"Does your mother keep you
warm at night, little one?"

"So does Mother Earth."

"Has your mother given you brothers and sisters, little one?"

"So has Mother Earth."

"Grandma, do you love
Mother Earth?"

"Yes, little one...

the earth is my mother."

"I love Mother Earth, too,
Grandma, just like I love
you and Mama."